A Family Garden of Christian Virtues

A Family Garden
of
Christian
Virtues

Susan Lawrence

SAINT LOUIS

To Mom, who planted the seeds
of God's Word in my heart

Copyright ©1996 Concordia Publishing House
3558 S. Jefferson Avenue, St. Louis, MO 63118-3968
Manufactured in the United States of America

Library of Congress Cataloging-in-Publication Data

Lawrence, Susan, 1950-
    A family garden of Christian virtues / Susan Lawrence.
       p.   cm.
    ISBN 0-570-04875-3
    1. Christian ethics. 2. Virtues. I. Title.
BJ1231.L38 1996
249--dc2o   96-19022
                                           CIP

2 3 4 5 6 7 8 9 10   05 04 03 02 01 00 99 98 97

Contents

As You Begin   9

My Own Sheep   11
New Clothes   12
How Do You Smell?   13
Lighting Our Path   14
Helping Heal the Hurts   15
Wonderful Fruits   16
Being Pleased   17
Pure or Dirty?   18
Gifts for a King   19
Your Attention, Please!   20
Bragging and Boasting   21
Promises   22
Testing, Testing   23
Walking the Path   24
An Awesome Fire   25
Secret Gifts   26
Spiritual Food   27
Surrounded by Enemies   28
The Best Combination: Faith and Works   29
Prized Possessions   30
Rules of the Tent   31
What Makes Us Unclean?   32
What Is That around Your Neck?   33

Praying for Enemies? 34
Giving All You Have 35
Two Kinds of People 36
Powerful Changes 37
Do Not Worry 38
Are You Humble? 39
What Can Separate Us? 40
I Thank God for You 41
You May Stumble, But You Won't Fall 42
Just Ask! 43
Planting in Good Soil 44
Stone Pillows 45
Cross Training 46
Going Fishing 47
The Rich Fool 48
Clean Hearts 49
Hide and Seek 50
Are You Being Blown Away? 51
Sweeter than Honey 52
Too Young to Be Chosen? 53
Thirsty Souls 54
Are You Spoiled? 55
Loving Our Brothers and Sisters 56
Fair Trading 57
Our Shield 58
You May Be Smart, But Are You Wise? 59
From God to You 60
You Are God's Show-and-Tell 61

Is Your Life Stormy or Calm? 62
Keeping the Lines of Communication Open 63
One Body, Many Parts 64
Is Your Heart Cheerful? 65
Follow the Leader 66
Under His Wings 67
Listening and Doing 68
A Prayer Lesson 69
Too Little Food, Too Many People 70
God's Building Blocks 71
Lost and Found 72
A Holy Life Is Brought to You By ... 73
Our Awesome God 74
Packing for a Trip with Jesus 75
Pass the Salt, Please 76
Preparing a Special Place 77
Our Road Map 78
Reduce Speed ... Anger Ahead 79
Shining Bright 80
Does God Ever Sleep? 81
The Vine and the Branches 82
Are You Ready? 83
Seven Detestable Things 84
What Is in God's Toolbox? 85
Whom Will You Serve? 86
"Fixing" God's Word 87
Praise the Lord! 88
Love in Action 89

Is Your Tongue Twisted? 90
From Rocks to Doughnuts 91
Our Giant Direction Book 92
Are You Too Busy for Jesus? 93
Keeping Healthy—Body and Soul 94
Still under Construction 95
Can You Guess What God Is Thinking? 96
Cleaner than Clean 97
God's "Home Schooling" 98
His Majesty ... the Servant? 99
Do You Need a Bridle? 100
How Does Your Light Shine? 101
Counting Hairs 103
God's Vision 104
Solid Construction 105
V-I-C-T-O-R-Y 106
Extraordinarily Ordinary 107
God's Majestic Creation 108
The Same Yesterday, Today, Tomorrow 109
Christmas: To the World—From God 110
Easter: Celebrate the Empty Tomb 111

As You Begin

It is the desire of my heart that this book, *A Family Garden of Christian Virtues*, will be used to plant the seed of God's Word in many hearts, and like the seed in the parable of the sower, that God's Holy Spirit will cause it to sprout, grow, and flourish. God's true and perfect Word points us to Jesus, our Savior, and gives us comfort and hope in Him. Whether you intend to use this book for family devotions, children's sermons, or in a children's ministry, the activities and messages are for all ages.

The "tools" in these devotions are used to ready the "soil" of your children's minds and hearts to receive the seed of God's Word. Research has shown that children learn best through active learning. They need to see, hear, touch, smell, and taste to understand and remember what they learn. The "tools" in *A Family Garden of Christian Virtues* are designed to be handled by those participating. Before starting your devotion, gather the items listed as *Tools*.

Now you are ready to "prepare the soil." Don't rush. Let children and adults alike answer the questions, use the "tools," and share in the discussion. Planting the seed of God's Word is serious business, but it can and should be enjoyed by all. Encourage everyone to share their answers.

The heart of the devotion is "planting the seed." Because children have relatively short attention spans, the Scripture selections in *A Family Garden of Christian Virtues* are brief. Read the Scripture with your young child on your lap or let him or her stretch out on the floor—however your child listens best. It helps to locate and mark the passages beforehand. When there are questions, encourage everyone to answer, even the youngest child. Never be critical or tell a child the answer is "wrong." Instead, reread a verse or two and help the child to understand.

Your response to the Scripture reading is the "harvest." This is the time that your family or group has a chance to apply what they have heard. Allow time for the "harvest" and participate in it with your children. Prayer is the best way to close any time with God's Word. Keep your prayers brief and at the children's level of understanding. Let everyone share the responsibility of the closing prayer.

If you haven't established a regular devotion time with your family, I encourage you to do so. It will become the most rewarding time of all—time spent with your family and with God. Choose a time that will work for you—maybe at a mealtime, maybe at bedtime. Prepare yourself to be the leader by praying before everyone gathers. Then love, laugh, and learn God's Word with your children in *A Family Garden of Christian Virtues.*

Susan Lawrence

My Own Sheep

Tools: Use a marking pen to color two eyes on a cotton ball or a paper circle for everyone.

Preparing the Soil: *(Give each person a cotton ball.)* This is your sheep for today. You must pretend that it is real and care for it. What things will you need to do for your sheep?

Planting the Seed: David was a shepherd, a caretaker of sheep. He later became the king of Israel. He loved God very much and wrote many beautiful songs. One of the songs that he wrote tells how God cares for us just as a shepherd cares for his sheep. *(Read Psalm 23. Explain terms that are difficult for young children.)*

Can you name green pastures, or good things, that God provides? Does He provide still waters? Do you have a valley of shadows—some scary or unpleasant things that have happened? What does God promise when we walk through the valley? *(He will be with us and comfort us.)* Just as a good shepherd would give his life to protect his sheep, Jesus gave His life on the cross to win us life with Him.

Harvest: Thank God for His loving care and His salvation in Jesus. Care for and watch over your sheep for the rest of the day to remind you of God's constant care.

New Clothes

Tools: Two items of clothing, one item very worn and shabby, the other new and preferably stylish.

Preparing the Soil: Would you rather have a friend that wore this *(show worn clothing)* or this *(show new clothing)*? If someone came to church in this *(show worn clothing)*, would you sit by that person?

Planting the Seed: Do you know what *favoritism* is? Favoritism is giving someone special privileges that you don't give others. James wrote a letter to a church that warned against showing favoritism. Let's see what he said. *(Read James 2:1–9.)*

Are rich people or people who dress well any more important to God? No, God loves everyone just the same. When He looks at us, He sees us dressed in the love and forgiveness Jesus won for us on the cross.

Harvest: Ask God to give you the strength to resist the temptation to show favoritism. Hang the new clothing over the worn clothing where everyone can see it for a day. Let it remind you of Jesus' love, which covers you.

How Do You Smell?

Tools: A bottle of perfume, cologne, or aftershave.

Preparing the Soil: Would anyone like to wear some of this perfume? *(Put a small amount of perfume or cologne on the hand of those who volunteer.)* Do you smell good? Wherever you are today, people will smell a pleasant aroma, and it will be you!

Planting the Seed: Did you know that you can be like perfume all the time, every day? The Bible tells us that Christians are a perfume to other people. *(Read 2 Corinthians 2:14–17.)*

What is it that the Bible says we can spread like a sweet perfume? *(We can spread the Good News that Jesus came to be our Savior.)* Who are some of the people to whom you might be a perfume? What kinds of things make you a good perfume? a rotten perfume?

Harvest: Ask God to make you a fragrant perfume to those who do not yet know Jesus is their Savior.

Lighting Our Path

Tools: Flashlights.

Preparing the Soil: *(Darken the room and let every-one turn their flashlights on and off.)* Are you afraid of the dark? Would you walk down a strange street or a path in the middle of the night without a flashlight to guide you? What might happen?

Planting the Seed: Sometimes when we try to find our way through life or try to figure out what God would like us to do, we feel left "in the dark." But God gives us a "flashlight" to light our way. Listen closely to this Bible verse to find out what is a "lamp [for our] feet" and a "light [for our] path." *(Read Psalm 119:105.)*

Yes, God's Word is a "light [for our] path." It lights our way to heaven as we learn the Good News that Jesus gave His life to save us. Without God's Word to show us the way, we are certain to stumble. Just like a flash-light shows us a path when it's dark, God's love for us—Jesus—shines through the Bible and shows us the way to Him.

Harvest: When do you use God's "flashlight"? Share how you set aside time to read or listen to the Bible. Invite everyone to do the same. Thank God for His Word.

Helping Heal the Hurts

Tools: Small, plastic-strip bandages.

Preparing the Soil: Does anyone have a scratch or cut that needs a bandage? *(Young children usually find a place for you to put a bandage. If not, put a bandage on yourself.)*

Planting the Seed: Can you imagine finding someone that's hurt and not helping that person? In our Bible story, not just one person but two people refused to help a badly injured man. *(Read Luke 10:30–37.)*

The Samaritan showed the love of Jesus to the injured man. Sometimes, though, people are hurt in ways we can't see. Their feelings may be hurt or they may feel sad or angry inside. Do you know anyone that needs help? We all need help, and God has given us the best helper ever—Jesus. He helped us in a way no one else can—He died on the cross so our sins could be forgiven. And just as He rose on Easter, we will rise to live in heaven with Him.

Harvest: Ask God to help you share Jesus' love with someone who's hurting.

Wonderful Fruits

☀ **Tools:** Fruit prepared for eating.

※ **Preparing the Soil:** How did this grow? *(For each piece of fruit you have, discuss how it grew (on a tree, bush, or vine) and how and when it was harvested.)* Do you think this fruit came from a good tree *(or bush or vine)* or a bad one? Why?

▨ **Planting the Seed:** When Paul wrote a letter to a church in Galatia, he compared our actions as Christians to fruit. Let's read part of that letter from the Bible and see what those actions are. *(Read Galatians 5:22–25.)*

What is the fruit of the Spirit? With the help of the Holy Spirit, this wonderful fruit can be seen in our lives as we respond to the great love Jesus shared when He gave His life for us. He helps us show love, joy, peace, patience, kindness, goodness, faithfulness, gentleness, and self-control.

✺ **Harvest:** Ask God to help each of you produce the fruit of His Spirit in your lives. Share the edible fruit.

Being Pleased

Tools: Brief handwritten notes to everyone that describe something accomplished during the past week that pleased you.

Preparing the Soil: *(Allow everyone to read their note. Read the note to young children.)* Notes like these make us feel good. We like to know that something we have done pleases others.

Planting the Seed: Our story today is about a time when Jesus was told that He had done something pleasing. *(Read Matthew 3:13–17.)*

What did Jesus do that made God happy? *(He was baptized.)* What did God say to show that He was pleased with Jesus? *(This is My Son, whom I love; with Him I am well pleased.)* How would you feel if God said He was pleased with you? We can't please God on our own. But Jesus took away our sins when He died on the cross. In our Baptism, God says, "You are My forgiven child. I am pleased with you." Because Jesus died for us and rose again, we will go to heaven to be with God.

Harvest: Thank God for sending Jesus to make you pleasing to Him. Ask God to help you do things everyday that please Him.

Pure or Dirty?

Tools: A clear glass or jar, a spoon, and a small container of dirt.

Preparing the Soil: *(Show a glass of clean water.)* Would you like a drink of this water? *(Let volunteers take a drink.)* This water is good to drink. It's pure. *(Explain how drinking water is purified or tested. Then stir a large spoonful of dirt into the water.)* Now who wants a drink? Is the water good or pure?

Planting the Seed: Our bodies are cleaned or purified when God gives us the gift of faith in Jesus Christ, our Savior. Our bodies become very special. *(Read 1 Corinthians 3:16 and 6:19–20.)*

A temple is a very special place—a place where we worship God. When God gave us the Holy Spirit in our Baptism, our bodies became temples. Would you want to bring dirt into a temple? Certainly not, but sometimes we do. The "dirt" might be watching a TV show or movie that we shouldn't, reading a dirty book, telling a bad joke or talking unkindly about others, or using bad language. Don't spoon dirt into God's temple. Instead, ask God to help you "honor [Him] with your body."

Harvest: Ask God to forgive you for the times you've brought "dirt" into your "temple." Ask God to help you bring Him honor with your body.

Gifts for a King

Tools: During the next section, everyone will need to choose a special possession.

Preparing the Soil: If a king came to visit us today, what gift would you give him? *(Allow everyone to choose a personal item as a gift. Discuss what they chose and why.)*

Planting the Seed: You chose some great gifts for a king. Did you know that we have a king? The Bible tells us that God is our King. The Bible also tells us what He would like us to give to Him. Listen closely to find out what that is. *(Read Micah 6:6–8.)*

What are the gifts God wants from us? *(To act justly, to love mercy, and to walk humbly with Him.)* How can we "act justly"? How do we "love mercy"? How do we "walk humbly" with God? Only through God's gift of faith in Jesus are we able to do these things. Jesus takes away our sins and sends His Holy Spirit to empower us to give God the gifts He wants.

Harvest: What gift will you give God today? Ask God to help you act justly, love mercy, and walk humbly with Him.

Your Attention, Please!

Tools: A megaphone. You can make one by rolling a piece of paper into a cone and taping it.

Preparing the Soil: What are some different ways that I could get your attention? I might talk to you through a megaphone like this one. *(Call out the names of one or more family members.)* I have something important to tell you. Listen to me!

Planting the Seed: In our Bible story, God had something to say to a young boy named Samuel. He was probably about your age. He lived with a priest named Eli. Listen to how God got Samuel's attention. *(Read 1 Samuel 3:2–10.)*

What did God do? *(He called Samuel's name.)* What did Eli finally tell Samuel to do? *(Eli told Samuel to tell God that he was listening.)* God had an important message for Samuel to hear and to deliver to others. Samuel was faithful to God and did what He asked. God has a message for you to hear and to deliver to others. It's the message of saving faith through Jesus Christ. With God's help, you can be faithful and tell others about Jesus.

Harvest: What are some ways that God speaks to us? Ask God to help you listen when He speaks.

Bragging and Boasting

Tools: Newspaper ads for new or used cars.

Preparing the Soil: Let's look at these car ads and find our "dream" cars. *(Pass out ads and let everyone find their "dream" car. Read ads to younger children.)*

Planting the Seed: It's fun to imagine having a "dream" car. Some people even think that a certain car will make them "cool," powerful, or popular. In Bible times, people didn't have cars, but they still boasted or bragged about their vehicles. Listen to what they boasted about. *(Read Psalm 20:6–9.)*

What did they boast about? *(Their chariots and their horses.)* Do chariots, horses, or cars have anything to do with what kind of people we are? *(No.)* What does the writer or psalmist say we should boast about or trust in? *(The name of the Lord our God.)* We boast in the name of the Lord because He has saved us. The Bible says the most powerful name on earth or in heaven is *Jesus.* Isn't that wonderful news to share with others?

Harvest: Think of one way that you will share your faith in Jesus with others today. Ask God to help you "boast" about Jesus. Praise God for all the wonderful things He has done in your life.

Promises

Tools: Something that represents the current season (green or colored leaf, flower, snowball, etc.)

Preparing the Soil: *(Let everyone examine the seasonal item.)* What would happen if the seasons didn't change: winter to spring, spring to summer, summer to fall, fall to winter?

Planting the Seed: Do you remember the story of Noah? *(If necessary, briefly summarize the story.)* What did Noah build? *(An ark or big boat.)* Why did he build it? *(Because God told him that He was going to flood the whole earth.)* After the flood waters receded, God told Noah it was safe to leave the ark. God also made two promises. As I read, listen for the promises. *(Read Genesis 8:15–22.)*

What did God promise? *(He promised not to destroy the earth with a flood again. He promised there will always be cold and heat, summer and winter, and day and night.)* God also promised to send a Savior and He did— Jesus! God has promised us a place in heaven because we believe in Jesus. And we can trust God because God always keeps His promises!

Harvest: Share your favorite season and what you like to do during that season. Praise and thank God for the changing seasons.

13

Testing, Testing

Tools: A piece of paper and a sharpened pencil for everyone.

Preparing the Soil: *(Pass out paper and pencils.)* We're going to take a test today. I want each of you to do your own work—don't look on your neighbor's paper. I want you to think hard and do your best. Answer yes or no to question number 1: Do you love Jesus? *(Ask young children to answer orally.)* Okay, put your name on your paper and hand it to me.

Planting the Seed: Did you know that the Bible tells us to take a test? *(Read 2 Corinthians 13:5–10.)*

Why should we test ourselves? *(To see if we are in the faith.)* We need to test our actions all the time to see if we are living as God would like us to live. Unfortunately, we don't always do what God wants. We sin even when we try not to sin. That's why God sent Jesus to be our Savior. He never sinned. He took God's test for us and passed with "flying colors." When Jesus died on the cross and rose from the grave, our failing grades were wiped away. Because of God's gift of faith in Jesus, we are on God's honor roll.

Harvest: *(Pass back papers.)* Write "A+ God's Honor Roll" on your paper and display it on the refrigerator. Thank Jesus for passing God's test for you.

Walking the Path

Tools: Four or five yards of yarn, ribbon, or string.

Preparing the Soil: *(Lay yarn on the floor in a sharply curving path. Walk on yarn without stepping off. Then lay yarn in a straight line and walk on it.)* Which path was easier to walk, the crooked one or the straight one?

Planting the Seed: The Bible compares our lives to a path that can be crooked or straight. Who will make our path straight? *(Read Proverbs 3:5–6.)*

Yes, God makes our path straight. On our own, we would try to walk the crooked path. We'd make nothing but wrong turns. But God is looking out for us. He sent Jesus to walk the straight path for us, a path that led right to the cross. Jesus died for our sins, for all the times we wandered away from God's path. Through faith, we walk with Jesus on God's straight path to heaven.

Harvest: Ask God to forgive you for the times you've tried to walk the path without Him. Ask God to help you trust Him to keep you on the straight path. If time permits, glue the yarn on construction paper and write Proverbs 3:5–6 below it. Hang it on a door, bulletin board, or wall.

An Awesome Fire

Tools: A candle and matches.

Preparing the Soil: *(Light candle.)* What happens to something in a fire?

Planting the Seed: Our Bible story is about a really awesome fire that didn't do what fires usually do. *(Read Exodus 3:1–12.)*

What happened to the bush that was on fire? *(It didn't burn.)* Who spoke to Moses from the fire? *(God.)* What did God ask Moses to do? *(Lead His people out of slavery.)* Moses listened to God and did what God asked him to do. Moses led God's people out of Egypt to the land that God had promised them. Although He could, God probably won't speak to us from the candle's flame, but He does speak to us through the Bible. God's Holy Spirit helps us read and listen to His Word and learn about the gift of Jesus as our Savior who saves us from the slavery of sin. The Spirit helps us listen and do what God asks. What are some things God asks us to do in His Word?

Harvest: Ask God to help you obey His Word.

Secret Gifts

Tools: Wrap a small treat in newspaper for everyone to enjoy.

Preparing the Soil: Do you like secrets? I have a secret. I've wrapped something in newspaper for all of us. What do you think it could be?

Planting the Seed: Usually when we do something well, we tell someone about it, such as when we do well at school, or complete our chores, or when Mom and Dad do a good job at work. We want others to know when we've done a good job. Jesus tells us, though, that sometimes we should do things and not tell anyone. Let's read and find out what they are. *(Read Matthew 6:1–6.)*

What things should we do in secret? *(Giving and praying. If your Bible translation says "alms," explain that it means giving money to the poor.)* Rewards and thank yous are nice but that isn't why we help others. We help others because Jesus first loved and helped us and has made us His followers. We don't want to keep the love of Jesus secret. With God's help, we share His love with others.

Harvest: As you share the wrapped treat, discuss things you could do secretly out of love *(make beds, do someone's chores, pick up someone's toys)*. Ask God to help you show love to others.

Spiritual Food

🌀 **Tools:** Small glass (or baby bottle) of milk for everyone and crackers or cookies.

🌿 **Preparing the Soil:** When you were a baby, what did you eat? *(If someone answers formula, explain that formula is like milk.)* As you got older, what kinds of food did you eat? What foods do you eat now?

◤ **Planting the Seed:** The Bible compares God's teachings to food. As I read, listen for the kinds of Bible food you are ready to eat. *(Read Hebrews 5:12–14.)*

Those who are just learning about God are like babies that need to drink milk. But as we grow as members of God's family, we need more food, solid food. We get to learn more and more things about God. God sends His Holy Spirit to help us grow in our Christian faith through reading the Bible and going to Sunday school and church. God's Spirit helps us live out our faith as we share the Good News of Jesus, our Savior.

⚙ **Harvest:** Share the milk and cookies or crackers. Ask God to help each of you grow in Christian faith.

Surrounded by Enemies

Tools: Dolls or small figurines—one for each family member. Six cans of food to represent "enemies." Use marking pens to draw angry faces on the cans. Set the dolls on the floor and surround them with the cans.

Preparing the Soil: Pretend that you are one of these dolls and that these cans are your enemies. How would you feel? *(Answers might include scared, angry, or hurt.)*

Planting the Seed: David was surrounded by enemies. King Saul had ordered these people to kill David. Listen to what David wrote and find out what David did when his enemies surrounded him. *(Read Psalm 27:1–5.)*

What did David do when his enemies surrounded him? *(He prayed and trusted in God.)* David knew the only person who could rescue him was the Lord. God rescues us too when our enemies surround us. God sent Jesus to defeat our strongest enemies—sin, death, and the devil. Jesus' victory is our victory. No matter what happens in our lives, we can say as David did, "The Lord is my light and my salvation—whom shall I fear?"

Harvest: Ask if anyone feels surrounded by enemies. Ask God to help those with specific problems and to keep everyone safe from their enemies. Memorize Psalm 27:1a.

The Best Combination: Faith and Works

Tools: Remove the "works" from a battery-operated or electronic toy or radio. If you can't remove the "works," remove the battery.

Preparing the Soil: Let's play with this. *(Attempt to make the toy work.)* Hey, what's wrong? *(Let everyone discover the toy has no "works" or battery.)* I guess a toy without its "works" can't do what it's really supposed to do.

Planting the Seed: Our Bible reading today tells us about our "works." Only God can look within us and see how strong our faith is. But others can see our faith in action when we share Jesus' love. Our *works* show that we are Jesus' followers. *(Read James 2:14–17.)*

When we don't share God's love with others, we are like the toy without its "works"—we aren't doing what God created us to do. Faith is more than just knowing about God. God's Holy Spirit helps us put our faith into action by helping others, just as Jesus did when He helped us by paying for our sins.

Harvest: Ask God to help you live out your faith by showing love to others. Make a plan to carry out your ideas.

Prized Possessions

Tools: Ask everyone to bring a favorite possession (toy, doll, etc.).

Preparing the Soil: *(Ask everyone to share their possession and why it is special.)* Almost everyone has "things" that are important to them. Sometimes these things become too important and keep us from doing what God asks.

Planting the Seed: Our story today is about a young man with a lot of things or possessions. He asked Jesus an important question. Listen for his question and Jesus' answer. *(Read Mark 10:17–23.)*

What did the young man ask Jesus? *(What must I do to inherit eternal life?)* How did Jesus answer him? *(Jesus told him to sell everything he had and give the money to the poor.)* Jesus doesn't tell us that having possessions is wrong. It's only wrong when the possessions become more important than our relationship with Jesus or get in the way of caring for others. Because of Jesus, God forgives us for the times we are more concerned with our possessions than with our faith. The Holy Spirit helps us put our most prized possession—Jesus—first in our lives.

Harvest: *(Hold hands for prayer.)* Take turns thanking God for something more valuable than your possessions. *(Jesus, family, friends, etc.)*

Rules of the Tent

Tools: Fold a piece of paper to make a "tent." Have additional paper and pencils.

Preparing the Soil: We all know about house rules, right? Whenever we go to someone's house, we obey their rules. This is God's tent. He gives us rules to follow as we live in His tent. Can you guess some of God's tent rules?

Planting the Seed: The Bible has a psalm or a song about God's tent rules. Let's find out what they are. *(Read Psalm 15.)*

What are the rules for living in God's tent? *(Do what is right, speak the truth, don't tell lies, don't do wrong to others, don't gossip, honor those who honor the Lord, keep promises, and don't take bribes. You might need to explain some of these rules, especially if you aren't reading from a children's Bible.)* We don't always obey God's tent rules. That's why we need Jesus. God sent Jesus to take the punishment for the rules we break. Because of God's gift of faith in Jesus, we can live eternally with God in heaven.

Harvest: *(Pass out the paper and pencils.)* Make your own tent and write some of God's tent rules on it. Now draw a cross over your list to remind you that Jesus has obeyed all God's tent rules for you. Put the tent where you will see it every day.

What Makes Us Unclean?

Tools: Various foods.

Preparing the Soil: *(Place the foods in front of you.)* Do any of these foods make us unfit to worship God?

Planting the Seed: A long time ago, the Israelites had a series of rules or laws concerning what they could and could not eat. When Jesus came, He told the people that there was an even greater law. Listen to see what Jesus said makes us unfit or "unclean" in God's eyes. *(Read Matthew 15:10–11, James 3:5–10.)*

What did Jesus say makes us unclean? *(What comes out of our mouths.)* What comes out of our mouths? *(Words.)* We all make mistakes. We gossip, swear, use unkind words, or speak in a disrespectful manner. When these words come out of our mouths, we are unclean—sinful. But God gives us faith in Jesus who washes away our sin. Because of Jesus, we are clean in God's eyes.

Harvest: Share the foods. Ask God to help you clean up your speech and use your words to share His love.

What Is That around Your Neck?

Tools: Yarn. Tricolor, uncooked skroodle pasta, cereal, or beads.

Preparing the Soil: *(Lay out supplies.)* Let's make necklaces! *(Allow family members to complete necklaces.)*

Planting the Seed: Our Bible reading today tells about something that can make us look as good as a beautiful necklace. *(Read Proverbs 1:8–9.)*

What is like an ornament around our necks? *(Our father's instruction and our mother's teaching.)* God gives us people who can help us learn more about Him and the salvation won for us by His Son, Jesus. He gives us teachers, pastors, and most important, parents to instruct and teach us His will. Just like a necklace makes you look special, the faith lessons you receive from your parents make you special to God.

Harvest: Ask God to help you follow your parents' teaching and instruction.

Praying for Enemies?

Tools: A pencil or crayon and paper for everyone.

Preparing the Soil: Draw a picture of someone that you love. *(Allow everyone to complete their drawings. Share the pictures.)* Let's pray for these people.

Planting the Seed: The Bible tells us that it is good to pray for the people we love. But they aren't the only people for whom we should pray. *(Read Matthew 5:43–44.)*

These verses tell us to pray for whom? *(Our enemies or those who persecute us.)* An enemy can be anyone we find difficult to love. It can be someone who treats us badly or even hurts us. Praying for our enemies is difficult! We were God's enemies because of our sin. But Jesus prays for us and even gave His life for us to win forgiveness for the times we fail to obey God's will. He helps us share love with others every day—even our enemies.

Harvest: Think of someone you consider an enemy. Ask God to help you pray for that person.

Giving All You Have

Tools: A penny, some paper currency, and a small box or container.

Preparing the Soil: *(Display money. Count it and discuss the amounts. Give the penny to one person. Place the paper currency in the box. Ask the person to put the penny in the box.)* I put all of this money in the box and *(name of person)* put this penny in the box. Who put more into the box?

Planting the Seed: In today's Bible story, Jesus was at the temple—a place of worship like our church is today. Jesus was watching the people put money into a container. *(Read Mark 12:41–44.)*

Who gave the most? *(The poor widow.)* How much did she give? *(Two small coins worth less than a penny.)* Why were the coins worth more than the large sums of money others gave? *(She gave all that she had.)* Jesus gave all He had—His life—for us. He came to earth, suffered, died, and rose from the dead. Now we share in the riches of eternal life. Whether we are rich or poor, Jesus helps us share our earthly and eternal treasures with others.

Harvest: Plan how you can be generous in sharing your blessings from God with others.

Two Kinds of People

Tools: Gather around a tree, preferably a full-grown tree that everyone can see. Collect a small amount of "chaff"—dry bits of grass or weeds.

Preparing the Soil: Which is stronger, this tree or these bits of chaff? *(Hold the chaff in your hand and blow it or let the wind blow it away.)* Would you rather be compared to the tree or the chaff?

Planting the Seed: Today we are going to read about two kinds of people. One is compared to a tree, and one is compared to chaff. *(Read Psalm 1.)*

Who is like a tree that is firmly planted by the stream? *(The person who doesn't walk in the counsel of the wicked.)* What does this person do? *(Delights in God's law and meditates on it day and night.)* Who is like the chaff that the wind drives away? *(The wicked person.)* We are rooted firmly in God's love. God keeps us standing straight in the death and resurrection of His Son, rather than being blown away like the chaff. Only with God's help can we make the right choices in life. With His help, we don't need to be like the chaff. We follow Jesus, the way to eternal life.

Harvest: Ask God to strengthen you through His Word and help you to choose friends carefully.

Powerful Changes

Tools: A glass of milk or water for everyone, spoons, and food coloring.

Preparing the Soil: What color milk would you like? *(Stir two or three drops of the desired food coloring in each person's glass.)*

Planting the Seed: We can change the color of our milk, but only Jesus has the power to change our hearts. In our story today, a man named Zacchaeus met Jesus. Zacchaeus was a tax collector. Like most tax collectors of that day, he cheated people out of their money. Meeting Jesus caused Zacchaeus to change. *(Read Luke 19:1–9.)*

What did Zacchaeus say he was going to do? *(He said he would give half his money to the poor and give back four times the amount to anyone he had cheated.)* Why did Zacchaeus decide to do this? *(Jesus had changed his heart.)* Jesus changes people through His perfect life of love and His suffering on the cross in our place. He has changed us from sinners into saints, from slaves to heirs of the kingdom of heaven. Jesus works in our hearts to change our sinful habits into loving habits.

Harvest: Think of bad habits that keep you from sharing Jesus' love with others. Ask God to forgive you and change your heart like He changed Zacchaeus.

Do Not Worry

Tools: Clothing catalogs or newspaper ads and scissors.

Preparing the Soil: Let's cut out pictures of clothing we like. *(Let everyone cut out one or two outfits. Share selections and why these clothes were chosen.)*

Planting the Seed: It's fun to look at pictures of clothes and choose the outfits we like. Today we are going to read what Jesus said about our clothes. *(Read Matthew 6:25–33.)*

What did Jesus say we shouldn't do? *(Worry or be anxious about what we wear.)* God provides all we need. God gives us food, a house, clothing, family, and friends. Most important, God clothes us in the forgiveness and salvation won by Jesus. What do we need to be concerned about? *(God's kingdom and His righteousness.)*

Harvest: Thank God for giving you everything that you need, especially for sending you a Savior.

Are You Humble?

Tools: None.

Preparing the Soil: I am the very best *(mom, dad, pastor, teacher, youth leader)* there ever was! I am the greatest! There never was another *(mom, dad, pastor, teacher, youth leader)* as terrific as I am! *(Pause for objections—unless your group is extremely polite, there will be objections or at least some weird looks.)* No one likes to hear someone brag, do they?

Planting the Seed: God doesn't want us to brag about ourselves either. Listen to what the Bible says about two men that went to the temple to pray. *(Read Luke 18:9–14.)*

Which man was justified or received God's forgiveness? *(The tax collector or the one who was a sinner.)* God reminds us that we are all sinners, that everyone makes mistakes. When we admit our mistakes, we are being humble. We know we need God to forgive our sins. We acknowledge that without Him we are powerless to deal with our sin.

Harvest: Ask God to make you humble and remind you of your need for a Savior.

What Can Separate Us?

Tools: Collect items that can be separated such as small blocks that snap together, pop-beads, or paper clips that are clipped together.

Preparing the Soil: *(Show everyone what you collected.)* Can you separate these? *(Ask one or two family members to separate the items.)* Was that easy or difficult?

Planting the Seed: The apostle Paul writes about something from which we who believe in Jesus as our Savior from sin can never be separated. *(Read Romans 8:35–39.)*

What is it that we cannot be separated from? *(God's love in Jesus our Lord!)* God's love is abundant and never ends. He loves us now and will love us forever.

Harvest: Thank God for His great love.

I Thank God for You

Tools: Pencils or crayons and paper for everyone.

Preparing the Soil: Name some people for whom you are thankful. *(Brainstorm for one to two minutes. Help everyone name someone.)* The Bible tells us to say thank you for many things, including people. People make a difference in our lives—by caring for us, by being our friend, or maybe by teaching us.

Planting the Seed: Paul often began his letters to the churches where he had taught by saying, "I thank God for you. ..." Listen to what he said to the people of the church at Philippi. *(Read Philippians 1:3–11.)*

Everyone must have looked forward to a letter from Paul. To know that someone thinks of us as a blessing makes us happy. As a result, we are more thankful for those who care about us. We see God's great care for us in giving His Son, Jesus, to be our Savior from sin. He is our greatest blessing.

Harvest: Write a brief note of thanks to someone who has been a blessing in your life. *(Ask young children to draw a picture or dictate a note.)* Thank God for His many blessings.

You May Stumble,
But You Won't Fall

Tools: Gather in an open area with enough space to try different ways of walking and hopping.

Preparing the Soil: Let's try some different ways of walking! *(Be creative. Give everyone a chance to lead. You might walk like a seal, a crab, use giant steps, and take baby steps.)* Now let's try some different ways of hopping. *(Hop on one foot, both feet, holding hands with someone, and without any support.)*

Planting the Seed: The Bible says that God knows our steps—whether we hop, take baby steps, or walk like a seal. In our Bible reading today, the psalm writer reminds us that God knows where we are going and goes there with us. *(Read Psalm 37:23–24.)*

What does God do? *(He makes our steps firm and holds us up when we stumble.)* Isn't that marvelous? Each day God guides us as we walk. We may stumble, but God won't let us fall. How comforting to know that even when we are having a horrible day, God is there, holding our hand, forgiving us when we stumble.

Harvest: Ask God to remind you that He is with you every day, holding your hand.

Just Ask!

Tools: A dish of candy, fruit, crackers, or any treat that everyone likes.

Preparing the Soil: *(While waiting for someone to ask for a treat, discuss a topic of your choice. As soon as someone asks for a treat, give it to him or her.)* Of course you may have one. Thank you for asking!

Planting the Seed: Our Bible reading today is about asking for things. *(Read Luke 11:9–13.)*

What do these verses tell us to do? *(Ask!)* This verse doesn't mean that God will automatically give us whatever we ask Him for. Some things we ask for aren't good for us. God has promised that whatever He gives us is right and good. God kept His promise to give us *all* that is right and good when He sent Jesus to be our Savior. God wants us to come to Him with our everyday needs. Remember we can always ask, and He will listen.

Harvest: Thank God for His good gifts and ask Him for help with any particular need.

Planting in Good Soil

Tools: Seeds (apple seeds, flower or vegetable seeds, or seeds from a weed), a container of rocks, and a container of dirt.

Preparing the Soil: Let's plant some seeds. We can plant some in this container and some in this one. *(Plant some of the seeds in the dirt and some in the rocks.)* In which container do you think the seeds will grow best?

Planting the Seed: Jesus told a story about a farmer who planted seeds just like we did. Listen to what happened to those seeds. *(Read Matthew 13:1–9, 18–23.)*

Which of the farmer's seeds grew best? *(Those planted in good soil.)* Jesus said that His words were like seeds. People who listened to His word and understood it were like what kind of soil? *(Good soil.)* God helps us to be like good soil. He planted faith in us at our Baptism and made us His children through the life and death of His Son. With His help, we listen to, understand, and share the Good News of Jesus with others.

Harvest: Ask God to help you listen to and understand His Word.

Stone Pillows

Tools: A stone or rock for everyone.

Preparing the Soil: I have new pillows for you. *(Give everyone a stone or rock.)* We've already taken your old pillows, so you can use these tonight. *(Allow time for protests.)* What do you mean, you don't think they would be comfortable?

Planting the Seed: In our Bible story, a man named Jacob used a stone pillow. While he slept, he had a wonderful dream in which God gave Him a promise. *(Read Genesis 28:10–17.)*

What did God promise Jacob? *(To give him and his descendants the land where he was sleeping, to be with him and protect him, to bless all people through his descendants.)* God kept His promises. The land eventually belonged to Jacob and his descendants, and many years later, Jesus was born, a descendant of Jacob and a blessing to all people. We don't have to sleep on a stone for God to give us a promise. The Bible is full of God's promises to us. The most special promise— God's promise to send a Savior—was fulfilled when Jesus was born. God keeps all His promises. He will be with us and protect us wherever we go.

Harvest: Thank God for all His promises. Memorize Genesis 28:15a together.

Cross Training

Tools: Wear workout clothes if possible. Pin or hang around your neck a sign that says "Coach." Blow a whistle, if you have one, to gather everyone.

Preparing the Soil: Everybody up! Let's do jumping jacks! One, two, three, four! *(Lead everyone in calisthenics—adults too!)* Doesn't that feel good? It's good for our bodies too.

Planting the Seed: It seems everyone is interested in staying fit. In Bible times, people wanted to stay in shape too. The Bible talks about the value of exercise. But it says that there's something else we need to keep fit. *(Read 1 Timothy 4:7b–8.)*

Besides physical training, what important training do we need? *(Training in godliness or spiritual exercise.)* Why is training in godliness so important? *(Because it has eternal value.)* Because spiritual training is so important, God is actively involved as our personal trainer or coach. With God's help, we effectively train in godliness when we read His Word, pray, worship Him, and witness about the forgiveness we receive through Jesus, our Savior. Thanks to God's help, we are on the winning team—the "Jesus Team."

Harvest: Think about how you take part in spiritual training. Ask God to help you keep your spirit "in shape."

Going Fishing

Tools: Some "fish" (fish crackers or paper fish) and a "net" (mesh fabric, tea strainer, or paper napkin).

Preparing the Soil: In the area where Jesus lived, there were a lot of fishermen. They used huge nets to scoop fish out of the sea. *(Demonstrate with your "fish" and "net.")*

Planting the Seed: Jesus wanted to teach His disciples another way to fish. In our story, listen for the names of the fishermen and how Jesus wanted them to fish. *(Read Matthew 4:18–22.)*

Who were the fishermen? *(Simon Peter, Andrew, James, and John.)* What did Jesus tell them He wanted them to catch? *(Men or people.)* Jesus wants us to be fishers of people too. We can share with others how God loves us so much that He sent His Son, Jesus, to die on the cross for our sins. Because Jesus took away our sins, we have the promise of eternal life. With God's help, we can catch many "fish" with this Good News.

Harvest: Share one way you can "fish for people." Ask God to help you on your "fishing trips." Share the fish crackers or color and display the paper ones.

The Rich Fool

Tools: A piggy bank, savings account ledger, or anything that represents saving money. Pencils and paper for everyone. As you begin, invite everyone to drop change into the bank.

Preparing the Soil: It's not only fun to save money, it's wise. By saving money, we can buy things that we would never have the money to buy otherwise.

Planting the Seed: Jesus warned us, however, against saving only for things that we can buy here on earth. He told a story about a farmer who did that. *(Read Luke 12:16–21.)*

What was this farmer's mistake? *(Saving only for himself and not having any concern for his eternal soul.)* We are not rich fools. We know we can't do anything to save our souls. Only God can save us. And God has a great "savings plan"—Jesus! Thanks to God's gift of faith in Jesus, our souls are saved eternally.

Harvest: Thank God for His wonderful "savings plan." *(Pass out pencils and paper.)* Write a prayer of thanksgiving on the paper. Then put it in the piggy bank.

Clean Hearts

Tools: Candy, plastic, paper, or fabric hearts.

Preparing the Soil: What type of heart would you like? Would you want a candy heart or a soft stuffed heart or maybe a golden heart?

Planting the Seed: When we do something wrong, when we sin, we need to ask for forgiveness. In the psalm that we are going to read today, the writer asks God for forgiveness and for something else. As you listen, keep track of what the writer wants from God. *(Read Psalm 51:1–4, 10–13.)*

What kind of a heart does the psalm writer want? *(A clean heart.)* The psalm writer knew that only God could wash away his sin and give him a clean heart. Thanks to Jesus' sacrifice on the cross, God gives us clean hearts too!

Harvest: Ask God to forgive your sins and give you trust in His promise of forgiveness. If time allows, cut out paper hearts and write Psalm 51:10 on them or share a treat of candy hearts.

Hide and Seek

Tools: Gather in an area large enough to play hide-and-seek.

Preparing the Soil: Let's play hide-and-seek. *(Choose someone to stay with you and count to 25 while everyone else hides. You and the counter search for everyone.)*

Planting the Seed: In the verses that we will read today, we are asked to "go seek." Listen and tell me whom we are to seek. *(Read Deuteronomy 4:29–30.)*

Whom are we to seek? *(The Lord our God.)* How will we find God? *(If we search for Him with all of our heart and soul.)* God never hides from us like all of you hid from *(person who counted)* and I. He is always there. When His Spirit leads us to seek forgiveness and love, He is waiting for us with open arms.

Harvest: Name some ways you search for God. *(Prayer, Bible study, Sunday school, church.)* Thank God for His presence.

Are You Being Blown Away?

Tools: A Ping-Pong ball, feather, or other lightweight object.

Preparing the Soil: *(Gather everyone around a table.)* Let's see who can blow this *(lightweight object)* off the table.

Planting the Seed: The Bible tells us not to be like this *(lightweight object)*, blown about by every new idea that comes along. Let's read to see how we can act instead. *(Read Ephesians 4:14–16.)*

What are some of the "winds" that we want to avoid? *(Older children understand the phrase "false doctrine" and can probably name some. For young children, discuss "truth" and "lies.")* How should we act instead? *(Like Jesus, building ourselves up in love.)* Our faith in the love and forgiveness we find on the cross of Jesus does not "sway in the wind." No wind, no matter how strong, can ever blow away God's gift of faith in Jesus.

Harvest: *(Weigh down the object with a Bible or heavy cross.)* This represents a Christian who is listening to Jesus. Try to blow the *(lightweight object)* off the table now. Ask God to help you avoid false teachings.

Sweeter than Honey

Tools: Crackers and honey or jelly.

Preparing the Soil: *(Give everyone a cracker with a little squirt of honey.)* Isn't this delicious? Do you think there's anything sweeter than honey?

Planting the Seed: The Bible tells us that there *is* something sweeter than honey. What is it? *(Read Psalm 19:7–10.)*

What is sweeter than honey? *(The law of the Lord.)* What is the law of the Lord? *(God's Word.)* What are some of the things that God's Word can do for us through the leading of His Spirit? *(Give strength, wisdom, happiness, and understanding.)* God has given us His Word because He wants us to know Jesus is the Savior of the world. God's promise of a Savior and His fulfillment of the promise are the heart of the Bible. Through this message, God blesses us with the "sweetness" of His Word.

Harvest: Ask God to make you "hungry" for His Word.

Too Young to Be Chosen?

Tools: Magazine or newspaper pictures of children and/or young people. Include pictures of your own children.

Preparing the Soil: *(As you discuss the following questions, point to individual pictures.)* Could God use these people to tell others about Him? Would He choose someone this age? How about this age?

Planting the Seed: A long time ago, God asked someone who was very young to tell others about Him. His name was Jeremiah. *(Read Jeremiah 1:4–10.)*

What did Jeremiah say when God asked him to help? *(He said he was too young and that he didn't know how to speak.)* What did God tell Jeremiah? *(He would help him and give him the words to speak.)* Jeremiah became a great prophet and for many years told the people of Israel what God said. God helps us speak just like He helped Jeremiah. When we tell others about Jesus' love and forgiveness, God is with us. He blesses what we say when we tell others Jesus is the way to heaven.

Harvest: Share one way you can tell others about God. Ask God to remind you that He is with you as you answer God's call in your life.

Thirsty Souls

Tools: A small glass of ice water for everyone.

Preparing the Soil: *(Encourage everyone to drink their water during the devotion.)* Can you imagine not being able to get a drink of water when you are thirsty? Our bodies need water to live. Wild animals need water too, and most of them live where they can drink from a pond or river or lake.

Planting the Seed: In the psalm reading today, the writer compares his need for God to a wild animal's need for water. What wild animal does the writer mention and why is the writer sad? *(Read Psalm 42.)*

What was the animal in this psalm? *(A deer.)* Why do you think the psalm writer was sad? How does this song or psalm end? *(With a reminder to hope in God.)* God is our hope and our help in any situation, even sinful situations. Because God gives us faith in Jesus, our sins are forgiven. We can always call on God to help us. There are times when we all feel sad, but if we desire God—just like the deer desires water—we will certainly be comforted.

Harvest: Praise God for His loving care each time you get a drink of water today.

Are You Spoiled?

Tools: Canned food, paper, and pencils.

Preparing the Soil: Why do we put food in a can and seal it? *(To keep it fresh.)* What would happen to the food if we opened the can and then put it back on the shelf? *(It would spoil.)*

Planting the Seed: There is a Bible verse that tells about a way to preserve our lives, a way to keep our lives from spoiling. *(Read Proverbs 13:3.)*

How can we preserve our lives? *(Guard our lips.)* How do we guard our lips? *(Think before we speak.)* What happens when we don't guard our lips? *(We might spread gossip, say unkind things, call someone names, speak rashly.)* When we speak rashly, it's like opening a can of food and putting it back on the shelf. We become spoiled. The only way to become "fresh" again is to ask Jesus to forgive us. With Jesus' love we will never "spoil."

Harvest: Share how God keeps you from "spoiling." Write your idea on a piece of paper and tape it to a can of food. Display the cans on a table or another place where you can see them often. Ask God to help you guard your lips.

Loving Our Brothers and Sisters

Tools: Some type of heart (drawn on paper, a heart pin, or clothes with a heart pattern).

Preparing the Soil: *(Point to a heart.)* What is this symbol? What does it mean?

Planting the Seed: What does it mean to love someone? Does it mean hugging and kissing? Let's read the Bible's definition of love. *(Read 1 Corinthians 13:4–6.)*

What does the Bible say about love? *(It is patient, kind, not jealous, etc.)* We show love by the way we act, by the things that we do and say. But *whom* are we supposed to love? *(Read 1 John 4:19–21. Insert "and sister" after brother.)*

God wants us to love our brothers and sisters. In this passage, "brother and sister" means our Christian brothers and sisters as well as the members of our family. At times we may not love our brother or sister as God commands. But God does not stop loving us. He shows His love by forgiving us because of Jesus. With God's help, we can love our brothers and sisters.

Harvest: Share one specific way you will demonstrate love to a brother or sister. *(Don't accept "be kind." Ask for specifics.)* Ask God to help you love your brothers and sisters.

Fair Trading

Tools: Baseball cards, stamps, or anything that everyone would recognize as something that is traded.

Preparing the Soil: If I were to give someone this baseball card *(or other item)*, what would I expect them to give me? What would I expect to get if I wanted to trade a valuable card? a worthless card?

Planting the Seed: Listen to what the Bible says about trading. *(Read 1 Peter 3:8–9.)*

These verses talk about trading evil and insults. Are we to trade equally—an insult for an insult? *(No.)* What does the Bible tell us to give back to someone who gives us evil or an insult? *(A blessing.)* A blessing can be anything that we do or say that helps someone feel God's love. God gives us many blessings, and He wants us to tell others about our greatest blessing—Jesus. Knowing Jesus loves and forgives us makes us happy. But more important, because of our faith in Jesus, we will live with God forever. God helps us trade blessings for insults.

Harvest: Plan how you will give a blessing when someone insults you. Ask God to help you trade blessings for insults.

Our Shield

Tools: A cardboard shield. *(Cut a circle from the side of a cereal box, a shirt box, etc. Decorate the shield and tape a handle on the back.)*

Preparing the Soil: Do you know what this is? *(If not, explain.)* A long time ago, men always went to war with their shields. What would the shield do for them? *(Protect them, keep them from getting hurt.)*

Planting the Seed: The psalm I'm going to read today compares God to a shield. *(Read Psalm 3:1–6.)*

How is God like a shield? *(He protects us. He sustains us. He keeps us from being afraid.)* The cross is our shield. Do you know why? Because Jesus' death and resurrection protects us from sin, death, and the devil. The Holy Spirit helps us call to God and trust in His love and forgiveness. Then, like David, we can sleep well, knowing God loves and protects us.

Harvest: Thank God for His protection. Make your own shield and write Psalm 3:3 on it.

You May Be Smart, But Are You Wise?

Tools: A treat such as crackers, raisins, or pieces of fruit.

Preparing the Soil: *(Eat some of the treat. Wait for someone to ask to have some.)* Of course, you may have some! *(Distribute treats to everyone.)*

Planting the Seed: Today's Bible verse tells us how God reacts when we ask for something. Listen to what we are to ask for and what God gives. *(Read James 1:5.)*

What should we ask of God? *(Wisdom.)* What will God give us? *(Wisdom.)* What is God's wisdom? *(Knowing Jesus as our Savior and living a life of Christian faith.)* How is it different than just being "smart"? *(Being smart doesn't save you from your sins. Only God's gift of faith in Jesus saves you and enables you to live a life of faith.)* God helps us grow into strong Christians. God gives us wisdom and helps us grow in faith.

Harvest: When do you need God's wisdom? *(All the time!)* Ask God to bless you with His wisdom.

From God to You

Tools: Wrap a special gift for everyone.

Preparing the Soil: Do we give a gift only when we think someone deserves one? We usually give gifts because we want to give someone something, not because the person deserves a gift.

Planting the Seed: God has a gift for each of us. Let's find out about God's gift. *(Read Romans 6:23.)*

When we sin, what do we deserve? *(Death.)* However, because Jesus died on the cross for us, we have a *free* gift from God. What is that free gift? *(Eternal life.)* When we believe in Jesus and know that He is the only one who can forgive our sins, then we are receiving God's gift of eternal life. God gives us the gift of eternal life through faith in Jesus.

Harvest: Thank God for His priceless gift of eternal life. Then unwrap your gift.

You Are God's Show-and-Tell

Tools: Pencils and two sheets of paper for everyone.

Preparing the Soil: *(Pass out pencils and paper.)* Let's draw a picture of God. *(Older children may protest that no one knows what God looks like; tell them they're right.)* Do we know what God looks like? Have any of us seen God?

Planting the Seed: The Bible tells us that even though no one can see God, there is something we can do to "show" God to others. What is it? *(Read 1 John 4:7–12.)*

What do we do to help others see God? *(Love one another.)* Love means helping and caring for others. Jesus is the best example of love. Jesus put our need for forgiveness first. He sacrificed Himself for us on the cross. Because of His great love, God helps us love others.

Harvest: Draw a picture of yourself. Then list ways that others can "see" God in you. Ask God to help you show love to others.

Is Your Life Stormy or Calm?

Tools: A large container of water and a small plastic boat or dish that will float in the water.

Preparing the Soil: *(Gather everyone around the container to make "waves." Discuss how the wind can cause large waves in a lake or sea.)* How would you feel if you were in that boat when the waves came up? What are some things that happen at work or school that are scary—like being in a little boat in a storm?

Planting the Seed: Jesus and His disciples were in a little boat in a big storm. Listen to what happened. *(Read Matthew 8:23–27.)*

Jesus' disciples were afraid because they didn't know that Jesus had power over the storm. Jesus has power not only over the storms in the sea, but the storms and scary times in our lives too. We don't need to be afraid of anything, including death or the devil. Jesus is Lord over *all.* Jesus is with us during all the "stormy" times in our lives.

Harvest: Think of someone you know who is facing a "storm." Ask God to calm him or her with His presence.

Keeping the Lines of Communication Open

Tools: A disconnected or unplugged phone.

Preparing the Soil: I'm going to call *(name a grandparent, relative, or friend. Dial the number and talk for a few seconds.)* They can't hear me! What's wrong? *(Someone should tell you that the phone is unplugged.)*

Planting the Seed: Talking to God is somewhat like making a phone call. We can't see Him, but we can talk and He will listen. But there is something that can break our connection with God. Just like an unplugged phone, it breaks our line of communication with God. *(Read Psalm 66:18–20.)*

What breaks our connection with God? *(When we have sin in our hearts.)* If we have sinned and refused to acknowledge and confess our sin, we aren't being honest with God and ourselves. God's Holy Spirit leads us to feel sorry for our sin and reminds us of the Good News that Jesus died to pay the price for our sins. We can trust God to hear us and forgive our sins.

Harvest: Plug in the phone and call someone special. Thank God for always listening to your calls.

One Body, Many Parts

Tools: A small ball or round object colored to resemble an eyeball. Pencils and paper for everyone.

Preparing the Soil: This eyeball is Fred. This is all there is to Fred. What kind of problems do you think Fred has?

Planting the Seed: In a letter to the church in Corinth, the apostle Paul used an eyeball to teach people about working together. Listen to find out what the Bible tells us about working together. *(Read 1 Corinthians 12:14–30.)*

When a church or group of Christians works together, they are like a strong, healthy body. Is any part of the body more important than another? *(No. They all work together.)* We are all the body of Jesus. Each one of us is a special part. We need each other. With God's help, we can work together to love and care for one another and tell the world that Jesus is our Savior.

Harvest: *(Pass out pencils and paper.)* Think of your own special talents. How are they like a part of the body? Draw your "body part." *(A person who serves others might draw a hand. A person who sings might draw a mouth, or a nursery worker might draw a heart.)* Ask God for help as you and your fellow body members work together to share the Good News with others.

Is Your Heart Cheerful?

Tools: A medicine bottle, jar, or container and a joke book or the newspaper comics.

Preparing the Soil: What is medicine used for? *(To heal people or to make us feel better.)*

Planting the Seed: There is a verse in the Bible that tells us about something that is like good medicine. *(Read Proverbs 17:22.)*

What is like good medicine? *(A cheerful heart.)* That's right, a cheerful heart keeps us healthy. God likes it when we laugh and have a cheerful spirit. Even when things make us sad, we still can have joy because we know God loves and cares for us. When we think of how He sent His Son, Jesus, for us, we are joyful. With Jesus as our Savior, we can rejoice all the time. *(Read Nehemiah 8:10b. If your group knows the song "The Joy of the Lord," which is based on this verse, sing it.)*

Harvest: Read several appropriate jokes or cartoons and share God's gift of laughter. Thank God for giving you joy in Jesus.

Follow the Leader

Tools: None.

Preparing the Soil: Let's play follow the leader. *(Play follow the leader or Simon says. End the game seated and ready to listen.)*

Planting the Seed: After 40 years of wandering in the desert, the Israelites finally had reached the Promised Land. But Moses, who had led them all those years, wasn't going to lead them to their new home. God had chosen Joshua to take over for Moses. The Bible tells us what Moses said to Joshua. *(Read Deuteronomy 31:8.)*

This promise is for us too. And just as Joshua could trust God's promises, so can we. We have many leaders—teachers, coaches, parents, and even friends. Sometimes people make wise choices and are good leaders; sometimes they aren't. God is our leader. He never fails us or leaves us. He forgives our sins, and He will lead us to heaven through the life and death of His Son. God helps us to follow Him.

Harvest: Who's your leader? *(God!)* Ask God to remind you of His promises and help you to be His follower.

Under His Wings

Tools: A feather for everyone.

Preparing the Soil: Pretend you are a tiny baby bird in a nest that's high up in a tree. Suddenly, danger appears—maybe it's a cat or a storm. Where will you hide?

Planting the Seed: Baby birds hide under the protection of their parents' wings. The writer of Psalm 91 describes how those who trust in God are protected. *(Read Psalm 91. Then reread verse 4.)*

Unlike the baby bird, we can't actually crawl under God's "wings." However, we can pray and trust that God is there to care for and protect us. Just as a baby bird clings to its parents for salvation from danger, we cling to God for salvation from sin. God's "wings" of love surround us with saving faith in Jesus.

Harvest: Carry the feather with you as a reminder of God's protection. Thank God for His protection.

Listening and Doing

Tools: A pitcher of a favorite beverage and glasses for everyone. Place these items within in sight of where you will gather.

Preparing the Soil: Would you like a glass of *(name of beverage)*? I would too! A glass of *(name of beverage)* would taste good right now. It would be so cold *(or hot)*, and I would really like it. *(Continue talking about how good your beverage is until someone notices the pitcher. Ask someone to pour a glass for everyone.)*

Planting the Seed: Wasn't it silly when I kept talking about *(name of beverage)* instead of just serving it? The Bible says we sometimes do the same thing with God's Word. Listen. *(Read James 1:22–25.)*

It's good to hear God's Word, but after we hear it, we are to do what it says. What does God's Word say to do? *(Read Mark 16:15.)* With God's help, we can tell others the Good News that Jesus paid for our sins and won us eternal life. Just like the *(name of beverage)* in the pitcher, the real goodness of God's Word comes when we do something with it. God helps us to hear and do His Word.

Harvest: How will you be a "doer" of God's Word? Ask God to help you hear and do His Word.

A Prayer Lesson

Tools: If possible, collect a completed homework paper from everyone.

Preparing the Soil: *(Discuss what everyone is currently studying. Look at the papers together.)* If you could ask your teacher to teach you anything, what would you ask him or her to teach you?

Planting the Seed: Did you know that Jesus' disciples called Him "teacher"? Today we're going to read about something they asked their teacher. What do you think it was? Do you think He taught them? *(Read Luke 11:1–4.)*

What did the disciples ask Jesus to teach them? *(How to pray.)* We call the prayer Jesus gave His disciples the Lord's Prayer. Although it shouldn't be the only prayer we pray, it's a good one to memorize. First, we remember that God is holy, that He is God (hallowed be Your/Thy name). Then we ask for things we need (give us this day our daily bread). Next we ask for forgiveness (forgive us our sins/trespasses) and for protection from evil (lead us not into temptation). Isn't it great that Jesus taught us to pray?

Harvest: Pray the Lord's Prayer.

Too Little Food, Too Many People

Tools: One cracker, cookie, piece of dry cereal, or slice of bread. Place enough of the food item for everyone in the kitchen or a nearby area.

Preparing the Soil: Let's all share this. How can we divide it so we will all get a share? *(Someone should protest that there isn't enough or that it isn't large enough.)*

Planting the Seed: Our Bible story tells about a time when Jesus had the same problem—too little food and too many people. *(Read John 6:1–14.)*

How much food did they have? *(Five loaves and two fish.)* How many people were fed with five loaves and two fish? *(Five thousand.)* How much food was left over? *(Twelve baskets.)* The feeding of 5,000 people was one of Jesus' many miracles. Jesus is God's Son. He is master over time, distance, sickness, sin, and death. He feeds us through God's Word, telling us how He died to win us forgiveness. The Holy Spirit gives us faith in Jesus and gives us the power to live according to God's will. God provides for all our needs and uses our small gifts to do great things.

Harvest: Thank God for giving you faith in His Son. Pass out the rest of the food item you had placed nearby and thank God for giving you what you need.

God's Building Blocks

Tools: A set of blocks, small books, or boxes. Provide a fist-sized rock and marking pens for everyone.

Preparing the Soil: *(Use blocks to build two adjoining walls.)* What will happen if I pull out this block that is the corner? *(Remove cornerstone.)*

Planting the Seed: A cornerstone is a very important part of a building. Even the Bible talks about cornerstones. *(Read 1 Peter 2:4–10.)*

Who is like a cornerstone? Yes, Jesus is the cornerstone, and we are the living stones. When our lives are built upon Jesus, we are strong in our knowledge that our sins are forgiven and we live in Him. We are being built into a special house—the church—made up of all people who believe in Jesus as their Savior. Without Jesus, what will happen? *(Indicate the fallen wall.)* God gives us faith in our cornerstone—Jesus.

Harvest: *(Pass out rocks and marking pens.)* How is Jesus the cornerstone of your life? Use the marking pens to write "Jesus is my cornerstone" on the rock. Keep the rock to remind you of Jesus' strength. Thank God for your saving faith.

Lost and Found

Tools: Candy, cookies, pennies, or another treat for everyone. Before beginning, hide one treat.

Preparing the Soil: *(Place the rest of the treats in front of you.)* Uh oh! I lost a *(name of treat)*. I must have dropped it on the floor. Please help me look for it. *(Wait for someone to find the treat and then gather the group.)* Why did you look for the one *(name of treat)* that was lost? Didn't we have enough? Why was the lost treat so important?

Planting the Seed: Once Jesus told His disciples a story about something that was lost. *(Read Luke 15:3–10.)*

What was lost? *(A sheep.)* Just as the sheep were important to the shepherd, we are important to our Good Shepherd. Every person is important to God. He doesn't want any of us to be lost in sin or not know the way to Him. Everyone in heaven rejoices when a lost sheep receives God's gift of forgiveness and faith in Jesus. No longer lost in a life of sin, the found sheep experiences love and forgiveness because of Jesus. We rejoiced when we found the lost treat. Imagine how God rejoices when He finds His lost sheep!

Harvest: Share the treats. Ask God to help you witness to a lost sheep.

A Holy Life Is Brought to You By ...

Tools: A microphone (a toy microphone or an empty toilet paper or paper towel tube).

Preparing the Soil: *(Use the microphone to announce: "This devotion is brought to you by [your name].")* TV announcers often say, "This program is brought to you by" and give the name of someone or something that supported the program. What is a sponsor? Did you know that you have a sponsor too?

Planting the Seed: The book of Colossians gives some important instructions about how we are to live our lives. It tells us that we are to give credit to our sponsor. *(Read Colossians 3:17.)*

Who is our sponsor? *(Jesus.)* Whatever we say or do, we do it all in Jesus' name. Could we disobey, be unkind, or mean in Jesus' name? *(No!)* Because God declares us holy by forgiving our sins, we are able to live a life in Jesus' name. He helps us act with compassion, kindness, humbleness, gentleness, and patience. God helps us live a holy life.

Harvest: Thank God for your sponsor, Jesus. Ask Him to help you lead a holy life.

Our Awesome God

Tools: Gather outdoors on a starlit night or use a photograph of the night sky. Star stickers.

Preparing the Soil: How many stars are in the sky? Could you count them?

Planting the Seed: God created the vast and beautiful expanse of stars in the night sky. What else has God done with all the stars? *(Read Psalm 147:1–11. Then reread verse 4.)*

What did He do? *(God counted and named all the stars!)* Even more awesome is that fact that God is our Creator, Savior, *and* Helper. We can trust Him to handle all our problems. He forgives all our sins and gives us eternal life through the life and death of His Son, Jesus. When we look at the night sky, we can remember all that our awesome God has done for us.

Harvest: Praise God for His awesome powers of creativity, salvation, and hope. *(Pass out star stickers.)* Wear a star sticker today to remind you of your awesome God.

Packing for a Trip with Jesus

Tools: Pencils or crayons and paper for everyone.

Preparing the Soil: Let's pretend that you are going on a trip. What would you take? Make a list of everything that you might need. *(For young children, help them draw pictures of what they would pack.)*

Planting the Seed: In our Bible reading today, we are going to read about a man named Matthew. Jesus asked Matthew to follow Him, to travel with Him. *(Read Luke 5:27–28.)*

What did Matthew take along? *(Matthew took nothing; he left everything.)* Why do you think Matthew did that? *(Read Philippians 4:19.)* Matthew trusted Jesus to supply everything he would need. We can trust Jesus to supply everything we need too. Sometimes the things we own can keep us from following Jesus. We may say, "If I only had that." But through the Holy Spirit's guidance, we can put away all the "things" of life and follow Jesus. He will give us everything we need—His love, His protection, His forgiveness—and keep us on track—all the way to heaven.

Harvest: What things might keep you from following Jesus or putting Him first in your life? Ask God to help you follow Jesus.

Pass the Salt, Please

Tools: Salty food (popcorn, saltine crackers, potato chips, french fries).

Preparing the Soil: *(Share the food.)* How would this taste if it didn't have salt on it? Would you rather have it with the salt or without? Do you think salt makes this better?

Planting the Seed: In today's Bible verse, Jesus is talking to His followers. He compares something to salt. What is it? *(Read Matthew 5:13.)*

What did Jesus say was the salt of the earth? *(Us!)* What does salt do for our food? *(Makes it taste better, gives it flavor.)* In the same way, we are to "flavor" the world. We make the world better with our Christian words and actions. God helps us to be the "salt of the earth." When we share the Good News of salvation through faith in Jesus, we "flavor" the world with the love of God.

Harvest: What's one way God can use you to "flavor" the world? Ask God to help you to be the "salt of the earth."

Preparing a Special Place

Tools: A feather duster or cleaning supplies—anything that you might use to prepare for company.

Preparing the Soil: If we had company coming today, what would we do to get ready? *(Discuss the common preparations you do for company.)*

Planting the Seed: Someone is preparing a place for us. Let's read in the Bible and find out who it is. *(Read John 14:1–7.)*

Who is preparing a place for us? *(Jesus.)* Where is this place? *(Heaven.)* We don't know exactly where heaven is, but we do know the way there. Jesus is the way to heaven. Although no one knows exactly what heaven is like, we do know that it's far more wonderful than we could ever imagine. Heaven is a wonderful place because we will be with Jesus. God shows us the way to heaven—and to Jesus!

Harvest: Use your own words to describe heaven. Praise and thank God for showing you the way to heaven.

Our Road Map

Tools: A road map—preferably one that shows where everyone lives.

Preparing the Soil: How would we travel to *(Name a town or area that everyone knows. Identify the roads that you would travel.)* A road map helps us get where we want to go. God has provided us with a type of "road map" too.

Planting the Seed: Listen to this prayer written by David. *(Read Psalm 25:4–6.)*

What does David want God to teach Him? *(His ways and His paths.)* How does God teach us His ways? *(Through the Bible.)* God's Word is like a road map. God gave it to us to get us where He wants us to be—in heaven with Him. The Bible teaches us that the way to heaven is through faith in Jesus, who lived and died for us. God's Word shows us where we have been (in sin), where we are (saved through faith in Jesus), and where we are going (to heaven). God guides us through His Word.

Harvest: In what direction does God want you to travel? Ask God to motivate you to read His Word and use it to direct your "travels."

Reduce Speed ... Anger Ahead

Tools: A large open area.

Preparing the Soil: *(Tell everyone to stand in a line facing you.)* Okay, walk as quickly as you can toward me. Now turn around and walk as slowly as you can. Touch your toes as quickly as you can. Now stretch up and down, touching your toes as slowly as you can.

Planting the Seed: Sometimes we do things quickly. Sometimes we do things slowly. The Bible reading today tells us one thing we should always do slowly. *(Read James 1:19–20.)*

What are we supposed to do slowly? *(Become angry.)* Why are we supposed to do this slowly? *(Anger won't help us live the righteous life God wants for us.)* Everyone has angry feelings. We need to talk about them and handle them in ways that won't hurt others. If we do lose our temper, we can ask God to forgive us. He will forgive us because of Jesus' sacrifice on the cross, and He will help us to be "slow to anger."

Harvest: What are some things you can ask God to help you do so you are "slow to anger"? Discuss some ways to handle anger appropriately and ask God to help you.

Shining Bright

Tools: A flashlight or small lamp and a box or object large enough to cover it.

Preparing the Soil: *(Turn off the lights. Turn on the flashlight or small lamp.)* Isn't this a bright light? It can really light up a dark place, can't it? *(Put the box over the light.)* I would be really foolish to have this bright light and cover it up, wouldn't I?

Planting the Seed: Jesus compares us to a light. Listen to what He says. *(Read Matthew 5:14–16.)*

Wherever a light shines, the darkness disappears. When we share the Good News of Jesus, our Savior, we are a bright light, chasing away the darkness of sin. Sometimes, however, we put the light under a box when we sin or neglect to share God's love. But God forgives our sin and keeps the light of Jesus' love shining in us. He helps us to be the "light of the world."

Harvest: What's one way you will let the love of Jesus shine? Sing "This Little Gospel Light of Mine." Ask God to help you to be a "light" in the world.

Does God Ever Sleep?

Tools: A bed pillow.

Preparing the Soil: I really like to sleep! If I put my head on this pillow and went to sleep right now, could I still see you? Would I know what you were doing?

Planting the Seed: Our awesome God has a wonderful characteristic. Let's read a psalm and see what it is. *(Read Psalm 121.)*

What does God never do? *(He never slumbers or sleeps.)* Isn't that remarkable? God will always take care of us, wherever we are, whatever we do, because He never has to take time off to sleep. God created us, saves us through the gift of His Son, sustains us, forgives us, and loves us. That's awesome!

Harvest: Thank God for His constant, loving care. Say a special bedtime prayer of thanks to God for staying awake to watch over you.

The Vine and the Branches

Tools: A large dead branch or stick.

Preparing the Soil: I'm going to lay this branch here until it grows leaves. Doesn't that sound like a good idea? *(You may need to explain that this is impossible.)* Why can't the stick grow leaves? *(It's dead. It isn't attached to the tree.)*

Planting the Seed: Jesus compared His followers to branches on a vine. How are you like a branch? *(Read John 15:1–12.)*

What does a branch need to live? *(It needs to be attached to the vine.)* We became attached to Jesus, our vine, in our Baptism. He gave His life to keep us growing in Him. He helps us live fruitful, productive lives. If we should live in sin, away from Jesus, we would be dead branches. But when we confess our sins, God forgives us because we are attached to Jesus. With His love and forgiveness, we produce fruit. Jesus helps us do and say things that please Him.

Harvest: Who helps you abide in Jesus? Break off a piece of the branch and thank Jesus for earning forgiveness for the times you act like a "dead branch." Ask Jesus to be near you always and to help you produce good fruit.

Are You Ready?

Tools: A suitcase or travel bag.

Preparing the Soil: What do I need to do to get ready for a trip?

Planting the Seed: When Jesus came back to life after His death on the cross, He spent some time with His followers. They were watching when He went back to heaven. Jesus made a promise. *(Read Acts 1:9–11.)*

What did Jesus promise? *(To return.)* Jesus promised He would return to earth! 1 Thessalonians tells us that no one knows when Jesus will return, but we will be ready for Him. *(Read 1 Thessalonians 4:16–5:6.)* Do we know when Jesus is coming? *(No.)* Should we pack some clothes to be ready for His return? God made us ready by letting Jesus die in our place to win us eternal life. God has "packed" our hearts with trust in Him. God gives us all we need through His gift of faith in Jesus. Because of our faith, we are always ready for Jesus' return.

Harvest: What is one way God is helping you prepare for Jesus' return? Thank God for His gift of faith in Jesus.

74

Seven Detestable Things

Tools: Pencils and paper for everyone.

Preparing the Soil: What do you hate? Make a list of (or draw) seven things that you hate. *(Let everyone share their list.)*

Planting the Seed: Did you know that God made a list of things that He hates? Listen for the seven things God hates. *(Read Proverbs 6:16–19.)*

What are the seven things that God hates? *(Haughtiness, lying, murder, wicked scheming, evil, false witness, and stirring up trouble.)* There are times when we are tempted to lie, cause trouble, or feel that we are better than others. We need to remember that these actions are sins—God hates it when we do these things. But when we sin, God works in our hearts to make us feel sorry for what we have done. Through faith in Jesus, God forgives our sins. Our names are written on God's "love list"—the book of eternal life.

Harvest: Ask God to help you avoid the seven detestable things and all sinful behaviors. Thank God for His loving forgiveness.

84

What Is in God's Toolbox?

Tools: Hand tools such as a hammer, screwdriver, or pliers.

Preparing the Soil: How do we use these tools? If I were to build something with these, would I need to know how to use them? What would happen to my project if I didn't know what tools to use or how to use the tools I had?

Planting the Seed: God provides us with some tools that we can use to tell others about Him. What is one tool we can use? *(Read 2 Timothy 2:15.)*

What is the word of truth? *(God's message of salvation.)* Where can we find God's message of salvation? *(In His Word.)* How can we handle it correctly? *(By knowing and reading the Bible.)* God gives us parents, teachers, and pastors to help us know and read the Bible. He also gives us another helper, the Holy Spirit, who helps us share God's Word with others through our words and actions. God helps us correctly handle His Word and tell others about the love He gave us in sending His Son to die in our place.

Harvest: What are you learning about the Bible? Thank God for His "toolbox"—the Bible.

Whom Will You Serve?

Tools: Crackers, raisins, or pieces of fruit for everyone.

Preparing the Soil: *(Ask everyone to choose a treat.)* We all make choices. Some are easy. Some are more difficult. What does it mean to make a choice?

Planting the Seed: After Moses died, God chose Joshua to lead the Israelites. Joshua led them into the Promised Land. There they learned some bad habits from their neighbors. Joshua told the Israelites that they needed to make a choice. *(Read Joshua 24:14–15.)*

What choice did Joshua ask the people to make? *(Choose whom they would serve—the gods of their neighbors or the Lord God.)* We don't have to make that choice. God chose us to be His children and sacrificed the life of His Son for us. But sometimes we may make ungodly choices and follow the crowd, even though we know it's sinful. Then it's time to remember who chose us. God chose us to be His children in our Baptism. God forgives our sinful choices and helps us serve Him.

Harvest: Pretend Joshua is asking you to choose whom you will serve. How will you answer? Thank God for choosing you and ask Him to help you serve Him.

"Fixing" God's Word

Tools: Yarn.

Preparing the Soil: Everyone do what I do. *(Sit, stand, walk, lie down. Finish by sitting, ready to listen.)*

Planting the Seed: What did we do? *(Walked, lay down, sat, stood.)* The Bible gives us some instructions about things God wants us to do while we walk, lie down, sit, or stand. What does God want us to do? *(Read Deuteronomy 11:18–19.)*

What are we to do with God's words? *(Fix them on our hearts, teach them to our children, and talk about them when we sit, walk, lie down, and get up.)* What are God's words? *(The Bible.)* The whole Bible is really about Jesus. It was written so that we would believe in Jesus and by believing we would have eternal life. In fact, Jesus Himself is the living Word of God. No matter what position we are in, God "fixes" His Word in our hearts and minds.

Harvest: What are your favorite words from the Bible? *(Pass out pieces of yarn.)* Tie this piece of yarn on your wrist to remind you how God's Word is bound in your heart. Thank God for His Word.

Praise the Lord!

Tools: Paper plates; beans, macaroni, or small pebbles; and a stapler. Crayons or marking pens are optional.

Preparing the Soil: We need to make noise today! Let's make tambourines. First, color the plates. *(This step is optional.)* Then place the beans *(macaroni or pebbles)* on one plate and lay the other over the beans. Now staple the plates together securely.

Planting the Seed: God loves us and helps us love Him in return. One way to show our love to God is by praising Him. Listen to all the types of praise that are suggested in this psalm. *(Read Psalm 150.)*

We have so many reasons to praise our all-powerful and great God. He created us and our world; He gives us all we need to live; and most important, He gives us faith in Jesus, our Savior. Now let's praise God with our tambourines!

Harvest: Sing your favorite songs of praise using your tambourines. Can you make up a new song to praise God? Praise and thank God for His great power and love!

Love in Action

Tools: Write a "love note" to each person.

Preparing the Soil: *(Pass out the notes and ask everyone to read their notes. Read the note to young children.)* Love notes are nice. What's another way I can tell you that I love you? *(Accept all answers but try to get the response that you could have "done" something to show your love.)*

Planting the Seed: Our Bible verse today is about loving others. How should we love others? *(Read 1 John 3:18.)*

Telling people that you love them is wonderful. But in addition to telling them, what does the Bible say to do? *(Show love with actions.)* Jesus loves in words and actions. He is the Living Word. Everything He did and said pointed to the great love He has for us. Then Jesus acted in love. He died on the cross to win us forgiveness for our sins. Now Jesus helps us show love to others.

Harvest: What's one way you will actively show love to someone? Ask Jesus to help you show love to others.

Is Your Tongue Twisted?

Tools: Collect some tongue twisters, such as "Susie sells seashells by the seashore"; "Rubber baby buggy bumpers"; or "Peter Piper picked a peck of pickled peppers."

Preparing the Soil: *(Ask everyone to attempt to say the tongue twisters. Start slowly and encourage everyone to go faster.)*

Planting the Seed: Tongue twisters are difficult. Our Bible reading today is about someone who couldn't speak well, even when he wasn't saying a tongue twister. Listen and find out who it was. *(Read Exodus 4:10–12.)*

God asked Moses to go to Pharaoh and to lead His people out of slavery. Moses thought he couldn't do it. Why? *(He wasn't a good speaker. He was slow of speech.)* What did God promise Moses? *(That He would be with Moses and teach him what to say.)* When God asks us to do something, such as tell others about Jesus and the forgiveness He won for us on the cross, He promises to be with us and help us.

Harvest: What's one thing God wants you to do? Remember, God will be with you and help you. Thank God for His help.

From Rocks to Doughnuts

Tools: Several stones.

Preparing the Soil: Pretend you are really hungry. What if someone told you he could turn these rocks into doughnuts but only if you became his slave. What would you say?

Planting the Seed: In our Bible story today, Jesus had a tricky conversation with Satan. Listen to what Jesus said to him. *(Read Matthew 4:1–11.)*

The devil was tempting Jesus—offering Him things that sounded good. The devil tempts us too. The devil tries to get each of us to do things that sound good but aren't what God wants us to do. How did Jesus answer the devil each time He was tempted? *(He quoted God's Word.)* We can answer the devil exactly the same way Jesus did—by telling the devil what the Bible says. The devil *hates* to hear God's Word. He knows that he was defeated for good when Jesus died for our sins and rose again. With Jesus, we can say, "Away from me, Satan."

Harvest: What is one thing that tempts you? Pray that you will be able to resist temptation. *(Pass out rocks.)* Keep this rock in your pocket today to remind you of what Jesus did when He was tempted. Ask God to help you resist temptation.

Our Giant Direction Book

Tools: Directions for a familiar game or toy.

Preparing the Soil: If you didn't know how to play this game *(or toy)*, how would you learn? What things would the directions tell you?

Planting the Seed: The Bible is our giant direction book. The best direction it tells us is how to get to heaven—through faith that Jesus gave His life for us on the cross. God's Word also tells us how to live a Christian life. In the passage we are going to read today, there are 14 specific directions. See how many you can remember. *(Read 1 Thessalonians 5:14–22.)*

What were some of the directions? Which directions do we need to follow? *(All of them.)* We aren't perfect. We can't follow God's directions without help. That's why we need Jesus. Because Jesus gave His life for our sins, God forgives us when we don't follow His directions. Jesus is like a "Get Out of Jail Free" card. Jesus frees us from our sin and gives us eternal life with Him.

Harvest: Share one of God's directions. Ask God to help you follow His directions and to forgive you when you don't. If time permits, you might want to play the game used as the "Tool."

Are You Too Busy for Jesus?

Tools: A snack. *(If you have devotions at mealtime, serve dessert; if you have them at breakfast, serve fruit or toast.)*

Preparing the Soil: *(Serve the snack. If possible, use special napkins or plates.)* It's fun to serve people and make them feel special. When we have company, do you like to help set the table and get the food ready, or do you like to spend time with the guests?

Planting the Seed: Our Bible story is about two sisters. One chose to serve, and the other spent time with her guest. Listen and find out who they were. *(Read Luke 10:38–42.)*

What was Martha doing? *(Preparing and serving.)* What was Mary doing? *(Listening to Jesus.)* What did Jesus say was most important? *(Listening to Him.)* Sometimes we are like Martha, too busy to listen to Jesus. But He forgives us and helps us slow down and listen to His Word. When we go to church or Sunday school, we are doing the most important thing—listening to God's Word. It's in God's Word that we learn about Jesus—the Living Word. He gave His life so that we may live with Him. Jesus helps us listen like Mary.

Harvest: Who is one person with whom you can spend special time this week? Ask God to help you spend time listening to Jesus.

Keeping Healthy—Body and Soul

Tools: Medicine (either prescription or over the counter, such as aspirin. Be careful with any medicine around young children.). Paper and crayons.

Preparing the Soil: What is this? When do we use it? Is there anything else that can help us stay healthy or regain our health if we are sick?

Planting the Seed: Listen to what the author of the book of Proverbs suggests for staying healthy. *(Read Proverbs 3:5–8.)*

What brings us healing? *(Trusting in the Lord.)* We've all heard of someone who was "worried sick." Sometimes we may even feel ill before a big test, an important game, or when making a big decision. When we pray for help, we trust God to answer us. His love heals our sick soul. Through Jesus, God has healed us from our worst sickness, the sickness of sin. He can heal our worried souls too. God keeps us healthy—body and soul.

Harvest: *(Pass out paper and crayons.)* Draw a large pill. Write Proverbs 3:5 or Proverbs 3:8 inside your pill. Thank God for healing your body and soul.

Still under Construction

🌀 **Tools:** An unfinished picture (person without face, animal without legs, house without roof), paper, and pencils or crayons.

🌾 **Preparing the Soil:** Do you like my picture? Do you think I've finished it? *(When everyone notices that it isn't finished, act surprised.)* Well, I'm still working on it.

🌑 **Planting the Seed:** Our Bible passage today tells us that God is still working on something, but He will finish it. Can you guess what it is? *(Allow guesses, then read Psalm 138:7–8.)*

On what is God still working? *(Us!)* God finished His work of saving us from sin when Jesus died on the cross. But God is still at work, caring for, protecting, and teaching each of us. Even grownups are still learning what God wants them to do and asking His help in learning how to do it. As His children, through faith in Jesus, God will keep His promise to take us to heaven. We can trust God to love us and guide us forever.

☀ **Harvest:** *(Pass out paper and pencils.)* Create an unfinished self-portrait and title it "God's still working on me." Thank God for His care and concern.

Can You Guess What God Is Thinking?

Tools: None.

Preparing the Soil: Let's play a game. I'm thinking of something in this room. What is it? *(Answer questions about the object until someone guesses what it is.)*

Planting the Seed: You're pretty good at guessing my thoughts. Our Bible passage today is about thoughts. *(Read Isaiah 55:6–9.)*

What does God say about His thoughts? *(They aren't our thoughts. They are higher than ours.)* Sometimes things happen to us or to others that we don't understand. Sometimes we pray for something and God's answer is the opposite of what we think it should be. When this happens, we need to remember that God loves us and always plans for our good. We know this because of what He has done for us in sending Jesus to die for our sins. We cannot guess what God is thinking, but we can trust Him, knowing He loves us.

Harvest: Share a time when it was difficult for you to understand why things happened the way they did. Ask God to help you trust Him to handle the tough times in your life.

Cleaner than Clean

Tools: Laundry detergent.

Preparing the Soil: What does this detergent do for our clothes? *(Read the promises of the manufacturer printed on the container, especially those about whitening or brightening.)*

Planting the Seed: In our Bible story, something happened to Jesus' clothes. Listen for what happened. *(Read Mark 9:2–8.)*

What happened to Jesus' clothes on the mountain? *(They became dazzling white.)* What else happened? *(God spoke and said Jesus was His Son and that we should listen to Him.)* This event is called the transfiguration. Can you imagine what it was like to be with Jesus like Peter, James, and John were? Our laundry detergent has things in it to clean our clothes, but there's nothing in here *(indicate box)* that will clean us on the inside from sin. The power for that kind of cleaning comes from the one who was on the mountain, the one of whom God says, "This is My Son. Listen to Him." Jesus died on the cross to win us forgiveness for our sins and to make us clean on the inside.

Harvest: Ask God to forgive your sins in the name of His Son, Jesus.

God's "Home Schooling"

Tools: Pencils or crayons and paper for everyone.

Preparing the Soil: Draw a picture of your father's house. *(Admire all the drawings.)*

Planting the Seed: Have you ever been lost? It can be really scary. In our Bible story today, a mother and father thought their child was lost. Listen to find out who the child was and where His parents found Him. *(Read Luke 2:41–52.)*

Who was the child? *(Jesus.)* How do you think His parents felt when they thought He was lost? Where was He? *(In the temple.)* Jesus was right where His Father in heaven wanted Him to be. Jesus was talking with the teachers there, preparing for the time when He would teach others about God's great love. This is a great lesson for us. We are never too young to go about the business of serving our heavenly Father. When we go to God's house, we hear the Good News that Jesus gave His life for us and we learn how to share that news with others. God guides and helps us as we live each day for our Savior.

Harvest: What are some things you learn at God's house? Ask God to bless your pastor and church teachers. Then ask God to help you learn more about Him and His will for your life.

His Majesty ... the Servant?

Tools: A tray or plate of crackers, fruit, or treats—enough for everyone—and napkins or small plates.

Preparing the Soil: Let's pretend that *(choose someone)* is a queen *(or king)*. Who would like to serve our queen *(or king)*? *(Someone serves the queen [or king] a snack.)* Do you think the queen *(or king)* is more important than the person who is serving her *(him)*?

Planting the Seed: Jesus told His disciples something that was difficult to understand. Listen. *(Read Matthew 20:25–28.)*

What did Jesus say we should do if we want to be great? *(Be everyone's servant.)* Although Jesus is the King of kings, He came from heaven to serve us by giving His life on the cross for our sins. He is the greatest servant of all.

Harvest: What's one way you will serve others? Serve the snack to one another. Thank Jesus for His service to us.

Do You Need a Bridle?

Tools: A toy horse with a bridle, a picture of a bridle, or if possible, a real bridle.

Preparing the Soil: *(Show the bridle.)* Do you know what this is? What is it's purpose? *(To guide or control the horse.)* What would happen if the horse wasn't wearing a bridle? *(It would go where it wanted, not where we wanted it to go.)*

Planting the Seed: God speaks to us in a psalm and tells us that we shouldn't be like a horse or mule. Listen to what God says. *(Read Psalm 32:8–10.)*

What does God want to do? *(Teach us the way we should go. Counsel us.)* We use a bridle to make the horse do what we want because animals don't understand. We aren't like a horse or mule. We can understand God's teachings. But sometimes we may be like a stubborn mule. We don't want to follow God's direction. God provides a Helper for us, the Holy Spirit, to lovingly guide us in our Christian faith. God's love surrounds us, leading us in the way we should go until is it time to live with Him in the home Jesus won for us.

Harvest: Share one way you can avoid being like a "mule." Thank God for the guidance of His Holy Spirit.

How Does Your Light Shine?

Tools: A small cardboard box (a shoe box works fine). Cut a quarter-size hole in one side. Place a flashlight or other small light inside the box. At the start, the flashlight should be in the box but turned off and the lid should be on the box.

Preparing the Soil: This box represents the world. Look inside and tell me what you see? *(Let everyone look inside and comment.)* Now I'm going to put a Christian in the world. *(Open the box and turn on the flashlight.)* What has happened to the world? *(Let everyone look inside and comment.)* God tells us that we are to reflect the light of our Savior and be a light to the world.

Planting the Seed: The Bible also tells us that how we act effects how our light shines. *(Read Philippians 2:14–16.)*

God reminds us that our light doesn't shine when we argue and complain. He forgives our complaining because of Jesus, and He empowers us to work with others without grumbling or arguing. With God's help, we reflect the light of Jesus, helping others to see Him as the Savior.

Harvest: What's one thing you often complain about? Ask God to help you "do everything without complaining or arguing." Think of something you can do today to let your light shine.

Counting Hairs

Tools: A small picture of everyone (if possible), glue, pencils, and paper.

Preparing the Soil: Guess what we're going to do. I want one of you to count how many hairs I have on my head! *(Someone should protest or young children may try.)* Do I have too many hairs to count? Okay, let's count *(name someone)* hair. Does *(name)* have too many hairs too?

Planting the Seed: Did you know that someone has counted the hairs on your head? Listen. *(Read Matthew 10:29–31.)*

Our God is an awesome God! He knows how many hairs *(name everyone)* have on their heads. But the really awesome part is that He loves and cares for each one of us so much that He sent His Son, Jesus, to die on the cross for our sins. Now we will have eternal life with our awesome God. We are worth more than anything else in the world. We are God's children and heirs of His kingdom.

Harvest: Glue your picture on a piece of paper (or draw a self-portrait) and write, "God has counted my hairs. I am valuable to Him." Praise your awesome God for His love and care.

God's Vision

Tools: Before the devotion, color two small pieces of paper to resemble eyes. Fasten them to the back of your head. You'll also need paper and crayons.

Preparing the Soil: Did you know that I have eyes in the back of my head? I do! Now I can see everything you do no matter where I am. Let's try them out. *(Everyone does something behind your back. You guess what it is.)* I guess the eyes in the back of my head don't work very well.

Planting the Seed: I know who truly sees all. Do you? Listen to our Bible reading. *(Read Psalm 139:1–12.)*

Because God always sees us, He cares for us and protects us. But there is one thing God does not look at. Because Jesus died to take the punishment for our sins, God no longer looks at them. Because of Jesus, God sees us as His forgiven children.

Harvest: *(Pass out paper and crayons.)* Draw and color an eye. Write Psalm 139:1–2 below your drawing. Thank God for His continual and loving presence.

Solid Construction

Tools: Building blocks or boxes or cans that will stack.

Preparing the Soil: Let's build a house. *(Build a small house with the blocks.)* What a house! Do you think this little house or the builders of the house *(point to everyone)* are more important?

Planting the Seed: The Bible tells us that the builder of a house is worthy of more glory than the house itself. God's Word is talking about a different kind of house. What kind of house is God talking about? *(Read Hebrews 3:3–6.)*

Describe the house. *(We are Jesus' house.)* Who is the builder of the house? *(Jesus.)* When others look at us, they are looking at a "house" built by Jesus. Our foundation is God's Word and Jesus is our Master Builder who saved us from our sin. The Holy Spirit continually reinforces our "frame" so we can stand against the storms of life. We trust God to give us courage and hope while we're "under construction." Someday our Master Builder's work will be complete, and we will be in His home—heaven.

Harvest: As a house built by Jesus, how will God help you share His "building plans" with others? Thank Jesus for being your Master Builder.

V-I-C-T-O-R-Y

Tools: A yardstick, broomstick, pole, or rod for everyone.

Preparing the Soil: Let's see how strong we are. *(Tell everyone to hold the stick above their heads with both arms until their arms get tired.)* That makes your arms tired, doesn't it?

Planting the Seed: In our Bible story today, Moses, God's helper who led the Israelites out of Egypt, had to hold a rod up. But his arms became tired. Listen to what happened. *(Read Exodus 17:8–13.)*

What happened in the battle when Moses' arms got tired and he put the rod down? *(The Israelites began to lose.)* How did Aaron and Hur solve the problem? *(They had Moses sit on a stone, and they helped him hold up the rod.)* God has won our most important battle for us. When God sent His Son, Jesus, to live a perfect life for us, die on the cross for our sins, and rise again, He won our victory over sin, death, and the devil. Now when the devil tempts us, God "holds up our arms" and helps us say, "You can't hurt me, Satan. Jesus already won my victory!"

Harvest: Name someone God uses to help you when you face a battle. Thank God for giving you the victory through Jesus Christ.

Extraordinarily Ordinary

Tools: A snack for everyone.

Preparing the Soil: *(Pass out the snack.)* Eating is such an ordinary thing. We do it several times each day.

Planting the Seed: In our Bible story today, Jesus tells a little girl's parents to bring her something to eat. But first Jesus did something extraordinary. *(Read Luke 8:40–42, 49–56.)*

What did Jesus do? *(He brought the little girl back to life.)* What did Jesus tell the girl's parents to do? *(Give her some food.)* When the girl ate, Jesus showed everyone their lives would be all right, even ordinary, again. Through this extraordinary event, Jesus' power brought a family back to normal from extraordinary grief. He has done the same thing for us by winning us the sure hope of eternal life with Him. When our lives are turned upside down and everything's going wrong, we can ask Jesus to help us. He's here, working to make things right, normal, and ordinary again.

Harvest: Thank God for His power to make things right.

God's Majestic Creation

Tools: Gather outside at night to observe the moon and stars. If this isn't possible, use a picture of the night sky.

Preparing the Soil: Just look at those stars and that moon. How wonderful to have their little lights at night. *(Spend some time stargazing.)*

Planting the Seed: Long ago David observed the moon and stars. But something else amazed him. *(Read Psalm 8:3–8.)*

What amazed David? *(That God thinks of us, cares for us, and crowns us with glory and majesty.)* The Creator of all the universe—the earth, the sun, the moon, the stars, the plants, and the animals—created us too. And He has put us in charge of everything He made. But what's even more amazing is that God loves us so much that He sent His only Son, Jesus, to be our Savior. We can share with others all the amazing things God has done.

Harvest: How can you be a good caretaker of God's amazing earth? Praise God for His majesty.

The Same Yesterday, Today, Tomorrow

Tools: Photo albums or pictures of those present (if possible) as babies, children, teens, and adults.

Preparing the Soil: Let's look at these pictures and see how we've changed. *(Look at the albums and discuss any changes.)*

Planting the Seed: The Bible tells us about some-one that never changes. *(Read Hebrews 13:8.)*

Who never changes? *(Jesus Christ.)* How wonderful to know that Jesus is always the same, always there for us—loving, caring, and forgiving. He never has grumpy days when He doesn't want to listen to us or days when He is too busy for us. Even though everything around us changes, and even though we change, Jesus never changes. He is always our Savior.

Harvest: Memorize Hebrews 13:8. Thank God for a Savior who never changes.

Christmas:
To the World—From God

Tools: A plastic, paper, or foil star.

Preparing the Soil: If you saw a star that was bigger and brighter than all the others, what would you do?

Planting the Seed: In our Bible story today, some men did see a star that was bigger and brighter than all the others. Let's find out what they did. *(Read Matthew 2:1–12.)*

Why did the men from the East follow the star? *(They were seeking the new king.)* These men followed a star for a great distance to find Jesus. We don't have to follow a star to find Jesus today. He came to us when we were baptized. The marvelous king that the men from the East knelt before and worshiped lives right in our own hearts.

Harvest: What gift can you bring to Jesus? Thank God for His gift of saving faith in Jesus.

Easter: Celebrate the Empty Tomb

Tools: Wrap a small, *empty* package for everyone. Place treats for everyone out of sight.

Preparing the Soil: *(Pass out the packages.)* Let's unwrap our packages. *(Give everyone time to react to the empty packages.)* How disappointing! You were expecting something special and the presents are empty.

Planting the Seed: Once some women found something empty that they thought held something special. *(Read Luke 24:1–9.)*

What was empty? *(Jesus' tomb.)* What did the women expect to be in the tomb? *(Jesus' dead body.)* Why wasn't He there? *(He had come back to life.)* This is the most marvelous story of all—that Jesus came back to life after dying for our sins! The empty tomb means we will have eternal life with God.

Harvest: *(Pass out the treats.)* Let's praise God for His Easter gift of eternal life.